T0195685

LIVE
LEARN
CREATE
RELATE

Okesene Temu Malala

WESTBOW
P R E S S®
A DIVISION OF THOMAS NELSON
& ZONDERVAN

WestBow Press books may be ordered through
booksellers or by contacting:

WestBow Press
A Division of Thomas Nelson & Zondervan
1663 Liberty Drive
Bloomington, IN 47403
www.westbowpress.com
1 (866) 928-1240

ISBN: 978-1-5127-4868-0 (sc)
ISBN: 978-1-5127-4869-7 (e)

Library of Congress Control Number: 2016910854

Print information available on the last page.

WestBow Press rev. date: 01/06/2017

CONTENTS

ACKNOWLEDGMENTS

I am indeed grateful to my foremost teacher the still small voice with the feeling communicated by the Spirit of the Lord. To speak the truth, without this great teacher I can't even been able to put this book project together. I spent many times trying to understand and seeking for the confirmation of the spirit for the right things to be written. It was hard when nobody believe that an ordinary uneducated man like me can do such a work. I'm very grateful for the gift of the Holy Ghost that throughout the whole project He has helped me organized and put everything in order.

It is very hard to work on some project that you never done it before or have any knowledge or understanding to do it, especially putting a book together without help from anyone, even your family don't even believe you can do it. My partner at the time, Sister Avau Pu'efua I wish you have faith since you heard the story who I am. But I have done it to prove to you that it is true who I am.

Very special thanks to my two daughters, Daisy Malala Latu and Leiloa Eseese Malala for their endless love and support. It's a great blessing to have you two in my life. To my back bone financial support for this book project Leiloa Eseese

Malala my younger and single daughter, much appreciated. Finally Dad has done it.

I dedicated this book to my grandchildren Yohana, Jahari, Dayton, Sadie and Kurt with my mother Leaiatuifanuaimeaatamali'i Lepou Malala who joined the church in the spirit world. To the late Sister Avau Pu'efua, my son OJ Malala and stepson Newman Manu, my testimony grew stronger and strengthen with many great lessons learned from our ups and downs. I have learned and understanded to be more patience from you guys.

I express my gratitude to Kate Lewis publishing consultant for convincing me to publish with WestBow Press. And to the whole WestBow Publishing team, thanks for the opportunity to rewrited the whole manuscript twice to correct all my own mistakes so I don't have to pay your kindly editing help which I thought its all included in the full payment that I made as I was told. Please accept my apologies. I am very humble to thank you and appreciated your great help and your patience. I have learned a great lesson. God bless.

This book is just a simple testimony gained and learned from the Restored Gospel of Jesus Christ but not an official statement of the church doctrine.

PREFACE

LIVE LEARN CREATE RELATE

**Have you ever ask yourself, "Where
did we come from? Why are we here?
Where are we going after this life?"**

This book is in a very simple english language, explaining
my knowledge and understanding with my sacred testimony
about what I have learned from the restored gospel of Jesus
Christ, where we came from, the purpose of life on earth
and how to find our way back to where we came from. This
book also focuses upon concepts, patterns and processes that
can help you and me learn for ourselves the fundamental
doctrines of the restored gospel of Jesus Christ on where
we came from, why we're here and where we're going after
this life.

The title of this book is from a small eight to ten pages
book written by my younger sister Alamaina as a project
when she was in high school in the early 1974. I had the
book with me in a long period of time, but I didn't even
paid any attention to its physical meaning until I joined
The Church of Jesus Christ of Latter Saint and started to

see the spiritual meaning that relate to the plan of salvation. When I started seriously learning the precept by precept of the restored gospel of Jesus Christ, this title clearly match up with the teaching of the plan of salvation and the answers to these questions.

- *Where Did We Come From?*
- *Why Are We Here?*
- *Where Are We Going After This Life?*

This book does not have a perfect knowledge answers approved by the church or its leaders but it's just a simple testimony received and a learned understanding gained from the restored gospel of Jesus Christ that I want to share to uplift and edify anyone who wants to learn the real truth. You will be surprise how simple this book can easily make you understand about the wise plan that God has for us, to learn about the place that we lived before we came to this earth, the purpose of life here on earth and where we go after this life after we die.

One thing I can promise you when you read this book, you will have the real feeling in your heart and mind. *"He will cause that your bosom shall burn within you, and therefore you shall feel it is right" (Doctrine & Covenants 9:8).* It is very interested to learn and understand the purpose of life that God our Father in Heaven has planned for us. It is a wise plan. You will also learn and understand that we did not just accidentally been here on earth.

If you read with a humble heart, and a willing desire to know and pay attention what the book is trying to explain, I promise you that your spiritual eyes will be open, your understanding will be more clearer and your learning will be increase when you learn and study the teachings of the restored gospel of Jesus Christ, and the teachings of its general authorities. (*The living prophets and apostles.*)

With these simple basic fundamental doctrines, I assure you, it will lead you to the true doctrine teaching of the restored gospel of Jesus Christ. The restored gospel of Jesus Christ is the Kingdom of God on earth, and it has the fullness of the gospel of Jesus Christ with the authority *(The Priesthood*) from God.

I have come to love these teachings that my understanding is more clearly now who I am, how important I am with the choices that I make in this life will benefit me in the next life. I have learned that this life is the time for us to prepare ourselves to meet our Savior and to learn as much as we can so we can be worthy enough to live with our Father in Heaven in his presence once again.

As I mentioned before, this is a very simple English language I'm using writing this book due to the very little education I have been blessed with, but I have come to know even more completely that the true and trustworthy teacher is the Holy Ghost. *"Who shall teach you all things, and bring all things to your remembrances" (John 14:26).* This Holy Ghost is the third member of the Godhead. With the associating of the companionship of this same Holy Ghost, together with some spiritual gifts and our individual responsibility to learn the doctrine of the kingdom. *"We may be instructed more perfectly in theory, in principle, in doctrine, in the law of the gospel, in all things that pertaining unto the kingdom of God, that are expedient for you to understand" (Doctrine & Covenants 88:77-78).*

I hope and pray that the combination of your faith in your Father in Heaven and the Savior, your willingness to study and the learning experiences in which you will engage, will invite the Holy Ghost to help you more fully understand basic gospel truths and a powerful spiritual pattern—at the end that each of us may LIVE, LEARN, CREATE and RELATE to our God who is our Heavenly Father.

CHAPTER 1

WHERE DID WE COME FROM?

When I was a little child, I was always believed that I came from my mother's womb because I was born in the hospital by a goodly mother in to this world. Like Nephi said, *"Having been born by goodly parents" (1 Nephi 1:1)*. It is correct in a sense, since it describe physical way we all came to the earth. Like our Savior Jesus Christ, who was born to this world physically by His mother and His father, Mary and Joseph. Mary and Joseph are His earthly parents, and they raised Him up the way the Lord commanded them through revelations and angel visitations until one day when they returned from the feast of the Passover in Jerusalem.

Jesus tarried behind in Jerusalem, and Joseph and Mary didn't know about this. After three days looking for Him. He was found in the temple sitting in the midst of doctors where He was both listening to them and asking them questions. When they found Him, His parents did not understand what was happening, and they asked Him why He was in the Temple. So He replied, *"How is it that ye sought me? Wist ye not that I must be about my Father's business?" (Luke 2:49)*.

God has once again spoken to men through His chosen living prophets in these latter-days: *"Surely the Lord God will do nothing, but he revealeth his secrets unto his servant the prophet" (Amos 3:7).* God from the beginning never changes; He was the same yesterday, today, tomorrow, and forever. *"For I am the Lord, I change not; therefore ye sons of Jacob are consumed" (Malachi 3:6). "Jesus Christ the same yesterday, and today, and forever" (Hebrews 13:8).* The true church of Jesus Christ and the authority of God were taken away from the earth after Jesus Christ and His apostles were killed, and a great universal apostasy occurred.

"And the woman fled into the wilderness, where she had a place prepared of God, that they should feed her there a thousand two hundred and threescore days" (Revelation 12:4-6). If there had been no apostasy, there would have been no need of a restoration. This same church and authority (priesthood) has been restored back on the earth and has the fullness of the gospel of Jesus Christ.

"And there shall rise up one mighty among them, who shall do much good, both in word and indeed, being an instrument in the hand of God, with exceeding faith, to work mighty wonders and do that thing which is great in the sight of God, unto the bringing to pass much restoration unto the house of Israel and unto the seed of thy brethren ... "That he has spoken unto the Jews, by the mouth of his holy prophets, even from the beginning down from generation to generation until the time comes that they shall be restored to the true church and fold of God; when they shall be gathered home to the lands of their inheritance,

2

and shall be established in all their lands of promise," (2 Nephi 3:24, 9:2).

This restored gospel of Jesus Christ is the Kingdom of God and The Church of Jesus Christ of Latter-days Saints on the earth. *"Set up a Kingdom, which shall never be destroyed" (Daniel 2:44)."Whom the heaven must receive until the times of restitution of all things, which God hath spoken by the mouth of all his holy prophets since the world began" (Acts 3:21).*Many of the truths of God and His gospel have been revealed through revelation to His living prophets. *"Surely the Lord God will do nothing, but he revealeth his secret unto his servants the prophets" (Amos 3:7).* It blesses us to understand that before we were born to the earth we lived with our heavenly Father in the pre-existence or the pre-mortal life.

"Ye were also in the beginning with the Father; that which Spirit, even the Spirit of truth … "Man was also in the beginning with God. Intelligence or the light of truth was not created or made neither indeed can be … "Even before they were born, they with many others received their first lessons in the world of spirit and were prepared to come to labor in his vineyard for the salvation of the souls of men," (Doctrine and Covenants 93:23, 29, 138:56).

After we experienced our spiritual birth, the Heavenly Father counseled and corrected us, and we were instructed, enlightened, and edified in His holy presence. God is the Father of our spirit. We are literally His children, and He loves us. We lived as spirit children of our Father in Heaven before we were born to this earth. *"Forasmuch then as we are*

3

the offspring of God" (Acts 17:29). "Shall we not much rather be in subjection unto the Father of spirits, and live?" (Hebrews 12:9). We were just spirits without a body of flesh and bones. We were not however, like our Heavenly Father, nor could we ever become like Him and enjoy all the blessings that He enjoys without the experience of living in mortality with a physical body. God the Father has a body that is a perfect body. *"The Father has a body of flesh and bones as tangible as man's; the Son also; but the Holy Ghost has not a body of flesh and bones, but is a personage of Spirit. Were it not so, the Holy Ghost could not dwell in us" (Doctrine and Covenants 130:22).*

When we were living with God in the pre-mortal life, we were all His righteous sons and daughters. And because we didn't have the opportunity or the free agency to choose otherwise, there was no evil, we did not make mistakes nor did we have any understanding of doing wrong. However, God's love for us made Him recognize that there was ultimately no happiness for all His spiritual children because they could not progress, learn, or make choices for themselves. So He decided to make a plan to help His sons and daughters to progress, be happy, and become just like Him.

So God made a plan, The Plan of Salvation:

"Now if it had not been for the plan of redemption, which was laid from the foundation of the world, there could have been no resurrection of the dead; but there was a plan of redemption laid, which shall bring to pass the resurrection of the dead, of which has been spoken ... "And they began from that time forth to call on his name; therefore God conversed with men, and

made known unto them the plan of redemption, which had been prepared from the foundation of the world; and this he made known unto them according to their faith and repentance and their holy works," (Alma 12:25, 30).

His plan is, He is going to make a world (Earth) to send down all His spiritual sons and daughters so that they could be tested. They would be able to learn and grow, and God would then be able to see if they would follow Him and do His will. And if they did, then they would be able to return to Him and live with Him in His presences again.

As a part of this plan, God wanted us to be able to receive a physical body so that we could learn to choose between right and wrong and to know good from evil; He also wanted us, to have the opportunity to become like Him by keeping His commandments and following the example of our Savior Jesus Christ. So coming to the earth is a blessing to all of us who accepted the plan when it was given to us in the premortal life for our sustaining vote to follow the plan when we come to the earth.

After God made the plan, there was a council in heaven: *"When the morning stars sang together, and all the sons of God shouted for joy" (Job 38:7).* The plan of salvation was presented to us before we were born to earth. *"And we will prove them herewith, to see if they will do all things whatsoever the Lord their God shall command them" (Abraham 3:22-26).* And God asked His Spirit children whom He should send to be our Savior. Satan came before God saying, *"Behold, here am I, sent me, I will be thy son, and I will redeem all man-kind, that one soul shall not be lost, and surely I will do it, wherefore give me thine honor." "But behold, my beloved Son, which was my Beloved and Chosen from the beginning, said unto me Father, thy will be done and the glory be thine forever" (Moses 4:1-2).*

Agency or the ability to choose is one of God's greatest gifts to His children. Our eternal progress depends on how we use this gift. Our heavenly Father chose Jesus to be our Savior, and He rejected Satan's offer because Satan wants to destroy human agency. *Satan ultimately, wants all the glory and honor of the Father, and he also wanted to change the plan. (Mose 4:3).* We must choose whether to follow Jesus Christ or to follow Satan.

After Jesus was chosen to be our Savior, Satan was very angry and rebelled against God. *"And there was a war in heaven, Michael and his angels fought against the dragon" (Revelation 12:7).* Two third of God's spirit children follow Jesus Christ, and one third of His spirit children follow Satan. Lucifer and his followers were cast out of heaven. *"And the great dragon was cast out" (Revelation 12:8-9).*

Satan and his followers will never be able to be born on the earth and have a physical body. *"And he became Satan, yea, even the devil, the father of all lies, to deceive and to blind men" (Moses 4:4).* Jesus has been chosen to be our Savior, and all of us who choose to follow Jesus in the pre-mortal life will get the opportunity to be born to the earth and receive a physical body. This body of flesh and bones will experience living in mortality so that we can learn to become like our Heavenly Father.

What would it be like if the blessings of the agency is taken away according to the plan of Lucifer? We would not have the chance to choose what we want because there would be no free agency for us to choose what we want at all. Because of our Savior Jesus Christ, we are so grateful and thankful for the blessing of having the free agency to choose for ourselves.

CHAPTER 2

WHEN WE WERE
BORN, WE LIVED.

Under the direction of the Father, Jesus Christ created earth as a place for us to live and gain experience. *"In the beginning God created heaven and earth" (Genesis 1:1)*. And man was also created by God in His own image. *"So God created man in his own image, in the image of God created he him, male and female created he them" (Genesis 1:27)*. *"And I, the Lord God, formed man from the dust of the ground and breath into his nostrils the breath of life" (Moses 3:7)*.

When we were born to the earth, we live. *"To live in this life, is to received a body of flesh and bones which is created in the image of God our Heavenly Father and already have the breath of life from Him."* Now we experienced our physical birth in mortality He desired to continue to communicate with us and to give us counsel and direction. As we live this life, we started out as little child that doesn't even remember anything from the pre-earth life where we came from.

We have earthly parents already prepared by our Heavenly Father to care and to raise us according to the plan that was presented to us in the pre-existence. These earthly parents are no different from the same roll that Joseph and Mary play as parent to our Savior Jesus Christ when He was born to the earth. Before we came to the earth we promised our Heavenly Father by raising our right hand in a square to show that we will sustain, obey, support and follow their righteous teachings.

It is very hard to remember anything from the pre-mortal life, because of the veil that block our memory from remembering every things that was given and taught to us in His presence. Sometimes we disobey our earthly parents by not remembering that we voted to come to the earth and obey them and follow whatever they teach us. In this life we live by faith. *"Faith without work is dead" (James 2:14, 20).*

The purpose of the restored gospel of Jesus Christ is to help us to remember and to understand how to live this earthly life and to follow the example of Christ who we follow and support in the pre-mortal life before we were born to the earth. We exercise faith in Him and repent of our sins. Then comes the remission of sins through baptism and by receiving the gift of the Holy Ghost from one who has the authority from God to perform these ordinances.

We then endure to the end; it means that we have to continue throughout our lives in exercising faith in Jesus Christ, repenting and renewing the covenants we have made with him through baptism every Sunday. These are not just steps that we experience once in our lives rather when repeated throughout life these principles become an increasingly rewarding pattern of living. In fact, it is the only way of living that will bring peace of conscience and enable Heavenly Father's children to return to live in His presence.

The blessings of been here on earth (*to live this earthly life*) comes from the choice that we make in the pre-existence to choose to follow Jesus Christ as our Savior when we come to earth. The restored gospel of Jesus Christ teaches us about the plan of salvation that gives us a clear true understanding about *how, why and what to* live on the earth. When we *live,* we should be none other than living for our Heavenly Father and our Savior Jesus Christ by following the plan of salvation, building up His Kingdom here on earth and live to become like Him.

With the physical body that we now have, we can help fulfill one important part of the plan of salvation, is to bring spirit children of our Heavenly Father to earth, to receive bodies of flesh and bones through marriage. Marriage is a commandment to every sons and daughters of God who come to earth. "*Let every man have his own wife, and every woman has her own husband*" (1Corinthians 7:2) *and the Proclamation to the world.*

Marriage is the opportunity to raise family, been able to have children, and become parents to *live* the way the Lord prepared for us. While we live in mortality (*earth*) we have experiences that bring us happiness. We also have experiences that bring us pain and sorrow, and some of which is caused by sinful acts of others. These experiences provide us opportunities to *live, learn and to grow,* to distinguish good from evil and to make choices. During our life on the earth each of us makes mistakes, we often yield to temptation and break God's commandments and sin.

Although it sometimes appears otherwise, sin always leads to unhappiness. Sin causes feeling of guilt and shame. Because of our sins, we are unable to return to live with Heavenly Father unless we are first forgiven and cleansed. Satan or the devil is an enemy to God's plan. God influences us to do good, Satan tempts us to commit sin. As with the physical death, we cannot overcome the effects of sin by ourselves. We are helpless without the Atonement of Jesus Christ.

When we grow up as a child, our earthly parent is responsible how we should live life, teaching us the Lord's way to be able to return back to our Heavenly Father's presence, setting good example for us to follow and helping us to use our agency properly to make right choices for ourselves. Some parents they have no understanding about *the purpose of life and God's plan for us,* so they don't care what kind of life a child will live.

In other words, when parents does not understand the true purpose of God's plan for life, a child that will be born to that family will have a hard time finding the truth to live and to return back to our Father in Heaven. And that will give a child the opportunity to start using his or her gift *the free agency* to make the wrong choices. Agency or the ability to choose is one of God's greatest gift to His children. Our eternal progression depends on how we use this gift. The *free agency* is given to us to choose what we want.

We must choose whether to follow Jesus Christ or follow Satan. We are free to choose anything of our choice or what we like. But in reality our Father in Heaven gave us the free agency to choose the right. Yes it's the freedom for us to choose but our Heavenly Father did not really want us to choose the wrong. When Satan tempted Adam and Eve to eat the forbidden fruit and they choose to do so. This was part of God's plan. Because of this choice, they were cast out from the garden and out of God's presence. This event is called the *fall* and *separation from God's presence* is spiritual death.

To *live* means, to live your whole life for our God, to love Him with all your heart, mind, might and strength. "*Love the Lord thy God with all your heart, mind, might and strength and in the name of Jesus Christ thou shalt serve him*" (*Deuteronomy 11:1, Doctrine and Covenants 59:5-6*). Jesus Christ is central to God's plan. Through His Atonement, Jesus Christ fulfilled His Father's purpose and made it possible for each of us to enjoy immortality and eternal life. Satan or the devil is an enemy to God's plan.

With the teaching of my mother and the learning from her church London Missionary Society (Protestant) helps me prepared to accept the learning of the restored gospel of Jesus Christ. I always thought to myself, to *live* this earthly life is just to enjoy living life here before you die. But now I learned from the restored gospel of Jesus Christ, to *live* this earthly life is to *live* the life that can return us back to Him and *live* like Him.

Obedience to Jesus Christ is a lifelong commitment. In order to live Christ like life we have to be truly and completely converted to our Savior and His gospel, through exercising faith, repenting, being baptized and committing to serve Christ, and then receiving the Holy Ghost, we can experience healing and forgiveness of our sins.

Jesus Christ set a great example, how to *live* life when He was on the earth. *"For I came down from heaven, not to do mine own will, but the will of him that sent me. And this is the will of him that sent me, that everyone which seeth the son and believeth on him may have everlasting life. And I will raise him up at the last day" (John 6:38, 40).*

When He was a child, His earthly parent Joseph and Mary was very worry looking for Him. *"Behold thy father and I have sought thee sorrowing, wist ye not that I must be about my Father's business?"(Luke 2:48-49).*

With the physical body that we have, we cannot live without physical food. When Jesus fasted forty days, He did eat nothing in those days, the devil tempted Him by saying unto Him, *"if thou be the son of God, command this stone that it be made bread ... "Jesus answered him saying, it is written, that man shall not live by bread alone, but by every word of God" (Luke 4:3-4).* This physical body we have is a Temple of God, which the spirit of God dwells in it. *"Know ye not that ye are the Temple of God, and that the spirit of God dwelleth in you" (1Corinthians 3:16, 1Corinthians 6:19).*

It is very clear that the body and the spirit both need to be fed physically and spiritually. The body is the instrument of the mind. In our emotions, the spirit and the body come closest to being one. What we learned spiritually depends to a degree on how you treat your body. That is why the word of wisdom is important. (*Doctrine and Covenants 89)*

The habit forming substances prohibited by that revelation tea, coffee, liquor, tobacco interfere with the delicate feeling of the spiritual communication, just as other addictive drug will do. Do not ignore the word of wisdom, for that may cost you the great treasure of knowledge even the hidden treasures promised to those who keep it. And good health is added blessing.

Also Jesus makes it clear the way the body and the spirit should live. No matter what the body wants, the spirit always leads. The spirit should always take control and the body should agree and follow. When the body takes control, the spirit withdrawal from the body. For example if the body wants to smoke, the spirit disagrees, and if the body smoke than the spirit leaves the body. "*If any man defile the temple of God, him shall God destroy" (1 Corinthians 3:17).* To *live* is to become like Him. And when *We LIVE We LEARN.*

CHAPTER 3

WHEN WE LIVE, WE LEARNED

The main purpose of God's plan for us to come to earth is to learn as much as we can to become more like Him and be able to return and live with Him in His presence once again. The Lord commanded us to actively *"seek learning, even by study and also by faith" (Doctrine and Covenants 88:118).* We seek learning not only because it is a commandment, we seek it because the desire to ask, to seek and to find answers to life's questions was planted in our hearts by our Heavenly Father. In order for us to understand the plan, we need to learn and act.

As learners, it is our responsibilities to learn, by asking, knocking, seeking and acting. As we learn our knowledge will increase and the eyes of our understanding will open. *"The fear of the Lord is the beginning of wisdom: and the knowledge of the Holy is understanding" (Proverb 9:10) "Learn of me and listen to my words, walk in the meekness of my spirit and you shall have peace in me" (Doctrine and Covenants 19:23).* I can remember the first learning from my mother when I was little, *"O ai na faia oe?" (who create you?)* Than we answer, *"O le Atua. (God).*

God wanted us to learn of Him and to know Him very well that He is the Father of our spirit. In order to have that wisdom, we have to have the knowledge and the confirming understanding about the Godheads. Remember when we left the presences of God to be born to the earth, we do not remember anything about God, where we came from, why we're here and where we're going after this life because of the veil that block our memory to remember anything from the pre-mortal life where we lived before we came to earth.

He wanted us to continually seek eternal truth, because this is central to how we come to know Him. Through sincere study of the restored gospel, we learned of the Father, the Son and the Holy Ghost. We learned who we are, and why we're here on the earth, and how we should live in order to enjoy happiness and peace in this life and a fullness of joy in the next.

To learn about the Godheads, they are three separated personages. *"Father and the son have a body of flesh and bones and the Holy Ghost is a personage of spirit" (Doctrine and Covenants 130:22).* Learning from the baptism of Jesus Christ, it makes it more cleared

1. Jesus was in the water
2. The Holy Ghost was descending like a dove upon Him.

3. Heaven was open Heavenly Father introduce Jesus. *"This is my beloved son, in whom I am well pleased"* *(Matthew 3:16-17; Mark 1:10-11).*

4. We believe in God the Eternal Father and His Son Jesus Christ and in the Holy Ghost. (Article of Faith 1)

Before Jesus Christ was received up into heaven and sat in the right hand of God, He gave His twelve disciples the authority (Priesthood). *"And I will give unto thee the keys of the Kingdom of Heaven, and what so ever thou shall bind on earth, shall be bound in heaven and what so ever thou shall loose on earth, shall loose in heaven"* *(Matthew16:19).* And He also commanded them, *"Go ye therefore, and teach all nations, baptizing them in the name of the father and of the Son, and of the Holy Ghost"* *(Matthew28:18-19).*

When the disciples were killed, this same authority (*The Priesthood*) Jesus Christ gave His disciples to preach the gospel is the authority of God given to all worthy men to bear, and act on His behalf on the earth was lost as the world understood. It was taken back by God. We learned from revelation given to John the beloved disciple of Jesus Christ, in the book of revelation he wrote;

"And his tail drew part of the stars of heaven, did cast them to the earth, the dragon stood before the woman which was ready to be delivered, for to devour her child as soon as it was born. And she brought forth a man child, who was to rule all nations with a rod of iron and her child was caught up unto God, and to his throne. And the woman fled into the wilderness, where

she hath a place prepared of God that they should feed her there a thousand two hundred and threescore days" (Revelation 12:4-6).

Now very clear what John saw in the revelation and gives us a clear understanding that the authority or the Priesthood of God was not lost or given to anyone. It was taken back by God. We learned the *woman* is the *gospel,* the *man child* that was borned is *the authority of the Priesthood.* The woman fled into the wilderness that she had place prepared of God means *the church was still on the earth but without the authority of God,* that they should feed her there a thousand two hundred and threescore days, *that is how long before the Priesthood authority was to restore back to the earth.*

We learned Jesus Christ and His disciple organized the church of God on the earth. When the disciples were killed and the true church Jesus Christ organized was lost because the authority of God was taken away from the earth and then the apostasy occurred. Men organized their own religion or churches according to their own understanding mingle with the scriptures. *"For behold, the darkness shall cover the earth, and gross darkness the people, but the Lord shall arise upon thee and his glory shall be seen upon thee" (Isaiah 60:2). "Wherefore the Lord said, forasmuch as this people draw near me with their mouth, and with their lips do honor me, but have removed their heart far from me, and their fear toward me is taught by precept of men" (Isaiah 29:13)*

The need for a Restoration

After the death of Jesus Christ and His Apostles, the power of the priesthood and many of the truth of the gospel were taken from the earth beginning a long period of spiritual darkness called the *Great Apostasy.* The prophet Amos of the Old Testament had prophetically foreseen this loss and pronounced that the time would come when there would be *"a famine in the land, not a famine of bread, nor a thirst for water but of hearing the words of the Lord" (Amos 8:11).*

During the long centuries of the Apostasy, many honest men and women sought the fullness of the gospel truth but were unable to find it. Clergymen of many faiths preached differing messages and called on men and women to join with them. Although most were honest in their intent, none had the faithfulness of the truth or the authority of God. However, the Lord in His mercy had promised that His gospel and priesthood power would one day be restored to the earth, and never to be taken away again.

With the wise plan of our God, it is that time once again the dispensation of the restoration is here, and the truth and the authority is needed to be restore as it was predicted. *"Repent ye therefore, and be converted, that your sins may be blotted out, when the times of refreshing shall come from the presence of the Lord. And he shall send Jesus Christ which before was preached unto you. Whom the heaven must receive until the times of restitution of all things, which God hath spoken by the mouth of all his holy prophets since the world began" (Act 3:19-21).* As the nineteenth century dawned, His promise

19

was about to be fulfilled and the long night *Apostasy* was about to end.

The Restoration

In the early 1800s, God was once again about to start the work of restoration back on the earth through a young boy name Joseph Smith as a prophet. Joseph Smith was borned in the year of our Lord one thousand eight hundred and five, on the twenty-third day of December, in the town of Sharon, Windsor county state of Vermont. As a young man, Joseph Smith assisted his family in cleaning land, hauling rocks, and performing multitudes of other duties. His mother Lucy reported that the boy Joseph was given to serious reflection and often thought about the welfare of his immortal soul. He was especially concerned about which of all churches proselyting in the Palmyra area was right. As he explained in his own words:

"During this time of great excitement my mind was called up to serious reflection and great uneasiness; but though my feelings were deep and often poignant, still I kept myself aloof from all these parties, though I attended their several meetings as often as occasion would permit. In process of time my mind became somewhat partial to the Methodist sect, and I felt some desire to be united with them, but so great were the confusion and strife among the different denominations, that it was impossible for a person young as I was, and so unacquainted with men and things, to come to any certain conclusion who was right and who was wrong."

"While I was laboring under the extreme difficulties caused by the contests of these parties of religionists, I was one day reading the Epistle of James, first chapter fifth verse, which read "*if any of you lack wisdom, let him ask of God, that giveth to all men liberally, and upbraideth not, and it shall be given him*"(James1:5).

"Never did any passage of scripture come with more power to the heart of man than this did at this time to mine. It seemed to enter with great force into every feeling of my heart. I reflected on it again and again, knowing that if any person needed wisdom from God, I did, for how to act I did not know, and unless I could get more wisdom than I then had, I would never know, for the teachers of religion of the different sects understood the same passages of scripture so differently as to destroy all confidence in settling the question by an appeal to the Bible."

"At length I came to conclusion that I must either remain in darkness and confusion, or else I must do as James directs, that is ask of God" (Joseph Smith—History 1:8, 11-13).

On a beautiful spring morning in 1820, alone in a grove of trees near his home, Joseph Smith knelt down and began to offer up the desires of his heart to God, asking for guidance. He described what then happened:

"Immediately I was seized upon by some power which entirely overcame me, and had such an astonishing influence over me as to bind my tongue so that I could not speak. Thick darkness

gathered around me, and it seemed to me for a time as if I were doomed to sudden destruction" (JS—H 1:15).

The adversary of all righteousness knew that Joseph had a great work to do and attempted to destroy him, but Joseph exerting all his powers, called upon God and was immediately delivered:

"At this moment of great alarm, I saw a pillar of light exactly over my head, above the brightness of the sun, which descended gradually until it fell upon me."

"It no sooner appeared than I found myself delivered from the enemy which held me bound. When the light rested upon me I saw two personages, whose brightness and glory defy all description, standing above me in the air. One of them spoke unto me, calling me by name and said, pointing to the other, this is My Beloved Son Hear Him" (JS—H 1:16-17).

As soon as Joseph again gained possession of himself, he asked the Lord which of all the religious sects was right and which he should join. The Lord answered that he must join *"none of them, for they were all wrong"* and *"all their creeds were an abomination in His sight."* He said that they had a *"form of godliness"* but they denied *"the power thereof"* *(JS—H 1:19).* He also told Joseph many more things.

After the vision ended, Joseph found that he was lying on his back, still looking into heaven. He gradually recovered his strength and returned home.

When the sun rose on that morning in 1820, Joseph Smith could scarcely have imagined that with the coming of twilight, a prophet would once more walk the earth. He, an obscure boy living in western New York, had been chosen by God to perform the marvelous work and wonder of restoring the gospel and the church of Jesus Christ to the earth. He had seen two divine personages and was now uniquely able to testify to the true nature of God the Father and His son Jesus Christ. That morning was truly the dawning of a brighter day—light had flooded a grove of trees, and God the Father and Jesus Christ had called a 14-year old boy to be their prophet. Quote from (Our heritage … Page 2-4).

Coming Forth of the Book of Mormon

Three years later after the visitation of God the Father and His Son Jesus Christ to Joseph Smith in the sacred grove, Joseph Smith prayed to the Lord for forgiveness of the follies of his youth and asked for further direction, after he learned himself he could scarcely have imagined that with the coming of twilight, a prophet would once more walk the earth and he himself as an obscure boy living in western New York, had been chosen by God to perform the marvelous work and wonder of restoring the gospel and the church to the earth. He had seen two divine personages and was now uniquely able to testify to the true nature of God the Father and His son, Jesus Christ. That morning was the truly the dawning of a brighter day-light had flooded a grove of trees, and God the Father and Jesus Christ had called a 14-year-old boy to be their prophet. The Lord answered by sending a heavenly messenger to instruct him. Joseph wrote;

"He called me by name, and said unto me that he was a messenger sent from the presence of God to me, and that his name was Moroni, that God had a work for me to do, and that my name should be for good and evil among all nations, and tongues or that it should be both good and evil spoken of among all people.

"He said there was a book deposited, written upon gold plates, giving and account of the former inhabitants of this continent, and the source from whence they sprang. He also said that the fullness of the everlasting Gospel was contained in it, as delivered by the Savior to the ancient inhabitants" (JS—H 1:33-34).

The angel (Moroni) directed Joseph to go to the hill, which was nearby, and told him many important things about the Lord's work in the latter days. He told Joseph that when he obtained the plates, he was not to show them to any person unless the Lord commanded him to do so. Joseph went to Hill Cumorah as instructed, and he said of this experience:

"On the west side of this hill, not far from the top, under a stone of considerable size, laid the plates, deposit in a stone box. This stone was thick and rounding in the middle on the upper side, and thinner toward the edges so that the middle part of it was visible above the ground, but the edge all around was covered with earth.

"Having removed the earth, I obtained a lever, which I go fixed under the edge of the stone, and with a little exertion raised it up. I looked in, and there indeed did I behold the plates, the

Urim and Thummim, and the breastplate, as stated by the messenger" (JS—H 1:51-52).

That is how the Book of Mormon came about as predicted in the Bible will go hand in hand with the Bible another testament of Jesus Christ. Ezekiel in the bible in the Old Testament bears witness that the stick of Judah is the (Bible) and the stick of Joseph is the (Book of Mormon). *"Moreover, thou son of man, take thee one stick, and write upon it, for Judah, and for the children of Israel his companions: then take another stick, and write upon it For Joseph, the stick of Ephraim and for all the house of Israel his companions: "And join them one to another into one stick; and they shall become one in thine hand. "And when the children of thy people shall speak unto thee, saying, Wilt thou not shew us what thou meanest by these? "Say unto them, Thus saith the Lord God; Behold, I will take the stick of Joseph, which is in the hand of Ephraim, and the tribes of Israel his fellows, and will put them with him, even with the stick of Judah, and make them one stick, and they shall be one in mine hand" (Ezekiel 37:16-19).*

Every time we go to court, it is very important that we have to have two or more witness, to prove the truth of what we testify of. The more witness we have, the more the judge or the jury will believe us. It is the same with testifying about Jesus the Christ. The bible and the witness of the Book of Mormon testify that Jesus is the Christ, the Savior and the Redeemer of the world, the only begotten Son of God, He died for the sins of the world, He was resurrected and He lives.

The Bible and the Book of Mormon both go hand in hand testifying about the birth, the mission, the death, the resurrection and the saving atonement of Jesus Christ to enable us to be saved. The ancients' prophets in the Old Testament in the Bible prophesy the coming forth of the Book of Mormon.

"Truth shall spring out of the earth; and righteousness shall look down from heaven" (Psalms 85:11). "And thou shalt be brought down and shall speak out of the ground, and thy speech shall be low out of the dust, and thy voice shall be, as of one that hath a familiar spirit, out of the ground, and thy speech shall whisper out of the dust" (Isaiah 29:4). " Moreover, thou son of man, take thee one stick, and write upon it, for Judah and for the children of Israel his companions: then take another stick, and write upon it, for Joseph the stick of Ephraim, and for all the house of Israel his companions." "And join them one to another into one stick: and they shall become one in thine hand" (Ezekiel 37:16-17).

The angel Moroni appeared and told Joseph to meet him at the hill in one year at that same time and to continue the yearly meetings until the time came to receive the plates. At each visit, Moroni gave further instructions about what the Lord was going to do and how His Kingdom was to be conducted (see JS—H 1:27-54).

Because of increasing persecution, Joseph and Oliver left Harmony and completed the work of translation at Peter Whitmer's farm in Fayette, New York, during June 1829. The completion of this work in the midst of such trying circumstances is truly a modern-day miracle. With little formal education, Joseph Smith dictated the translation in just a little over two months of actual working time and made very few corrections. The book stands today essentially as he translated it and has been the source of testimony for millions of people throughout the world. Joseph Smith was a powerful instrument in the hands of the Lord in bringing forth the words of ancient prophets for the blessing of Saints in the latter days. (Our Heritage page 9)

Witness to the Book of Mormon

While the Prophet Joseph Smith was in Fayette, the Lord revealed that Oliver Cowdery, David Whitmer and Martin Harris were to be three special witnesses who would be permitted to see the gold plates (see 2 Nephi 27:12; Ether 5:2-4; D&C 17). They along with Joseph would be able to testify of the origin and truth of this ancient record.

Joseph was blessed with the help of Oliver Cowdery, a young schoolteacher who was directed by the Lord to the prophet's home. Oliver commenced to write on 7 April 1829. Of that momentous time he said, *"These were days never to be forgotten—to sit under the sound of a voice dictated by the inspiration of heaven, awakened the utmost gratitude of his bosom!"* (JS—H 1:71, footnote).

Oliver further declared: *"That book is true ... I wrote it myself as it fell from the lips of the Prophet. It contains the everlasting gospel, and comes in fulfillment of the revelations of John where it says he saw an angel come with the everlasting gospel to preach* to every nation, tongue and people. It contains principles of salvation. And if you will walk by its light and obey its precepts you will be saved in the everlasting kingdom of God."

David Whitmer explained: *"We went into the woods, nearby and sat down on a log and talked awhile. We then kneeled down and prayed. We then got up and sat on the log and were talking, when all at once a light came down from above us and encircled us for quite a little distance around; and the angel stood before us."*

This angel was Moroni. David said that he *"was dressed in white, and spoke and called me by name and said, "Blessed is he that keepeth His commandments."* A table was set before us and on it the records were placed. The records of the Nephites, from which the Book of Mormon was translated, the brass plated, the ball of director, the sword of Laban, and other plates. While the men were viewing these things, they heard a voice that said: *"These plates have been revealed by the power of God, and they have been translated by the power of God. The translation of them which you have seen is correct, and I command you to bear record of what you now see and hear."*

Soon after this event, Joseph Smith shows the plates to eight additional witnesses, who handled them in a secluded setting near the smith family home in Manchester, New York. The testimonies of both groups of witnesses are recorded at the beginning of the Book of Mormon.

Restoration of the Aaronic and Melchizedek Priesthood

When the angel Moroni first met with Joseph Smith on the Hill Cumorah in September 1823, he gave important instructions about the restoration of the priesthood authority to the earth, including the following declaration: "When (the gold plates) are interpreted *the Lord will give the priesthood to some,* and they shall begin to proclaim this gospel and baptize by water, and after that they shall have power to give the Holy Ghost by laying of their hands."

In the spring of 1829 15, May on the bank of Susquehanna River, Joseph Smith and Oliver were visited by a heavenly messenger. He identify himself as John the Baptist of the New Testament times. Laying his hands on the heads of Joseph and Oliver, he said, *"upon you my fellow servants, in the name of the Messiah I confer the Priesthood of Aaron, which holds the keys of the ministering of angels, and of the gospel of repentance, and of baptism by immersion for the remission of sins"* (Doctrine and Covenants13:1).

Later Peter, James and John appeared to Joseph and Oliver and conferred upon them the Melchizedek Priesthood. They also bestowed the keys of God's Kingdom upon them *(Doctrine and Covenants 27:12-13; 128:20).* The Melchizedek Priesthood is the higher authority given to men on earth. With this authority, the prophet Joseph Smith was able to organize the Church of Jesus Christ of Latter-Saints in this dispensation and begin to establish the various priesthood quorums as they are known in the Church today. (see complete story ... Our Heritage)

Organization of the Church

Now with the Authority (The Priesthood) has been restored back on the earth, Peter, James and John appeared to Joseph Smith and Oliver Cowdery and conferred upon them the Melchizedek Priesthood and the Lord revealed to Joseph Smith that 6 April 1830 was the day on which the Church of Jesus Christ in this dispensation was to be organized (*Doctrine and Covenant 20:1).* This was the same church Jesus Christ organized and preaches with His disciples when they were on the earth.

When they were killed the church was taken away and now it is been restored back on earth and nothing has been change. God never change, he is the same yesterday, today and tomorrow. Joseph Smith was chosen by God to be the Prophet of the Restoration to restored the true Gospel of Jesus Christ back on the earth that has the fullness of the Gospel of our Father in Heaven. On the same year 1830 Joseph Smith organized the church under the direction of God the Father and His son Jesus Christ. The world heard of the true church has been restored and organized, than people start to preach and spread the word around, about the good news Jesus Christ and its true church has been organized and restored back on earth.

As recorded in the church history of the Samoan Islands and the Pacific Islands, a man name John Williams arrived in the

Pacific Islands in the year 1830 claiming that he is from God bringing the good news (the gospel) in the name of Jesus Christ for people to be saved. Than London Missionary Society (LMS or Loku Kaiki) and Methodist (Lotu Tonga or Metotisi) churches was organized. Many of the Samoan people became Christians by joining these religious group accepting the good news that Jesus can change and saves us from our sins.

Many have believed that John Williams is a man from God and a great spirit who came from God to bring the good news (*The Gospel*). When Samoan speeches are presented, it always mentions the important of this day, the day John Williams arrived with the gospel in Samoa. The morning of the arrival of the gospel in Samoa. (Le Taeao Na Taunu'u mai iai le Talalelei I Samoa).

Ever since the arrival of John Williams, the Samoan and the Pacific Island people stood steadfast to the belief that he preached, mingle with the scriptures (the bible) together with the belief and the teaching of men, and should be no other way until the first member of the restored gospel that was organized by Joseph Smith in the year of 1830, arrived in the Pacific Islands later after John Williams.

In June 21st 1888 Joseph Dean and his wife been called and sent from Hawaii arrived in Aunu'u as the first official missionary in Samoa in response to Manoa's request. (see Building of the Kingdom in Samoa Page 6-9) The restored gospel of Jesus Christ was established, further missionary work on Aunu'u was very successful, and the gospel spread to the Island of Tutuila and later to the Island of Upolu.

As we learned from the time of John the Baptist, John was the one who prepared the way of the coming of our Lord Jesus Christ. *"As it is written in the prophets, Behold, I sent my messenger before thy face, which shall prepare thy way before thee. The voice of one crying in the wilderness, Prepare ye the way of the Lord, make his paths straight" (Mark 1:2-3, Luke 3:4).*

With John the Baptist's preaching, it prepared people to accept He who will come after him. *"I indeed baptize you with water unto repentance, but he that comes after me is mightier than I, whose shoes I am not worthy to bear. He shall baptize you with the Holy Ghost and with fire" (Matthew 3:11).* When Jesus came, people who believed in John's preaching easily believe and follow Jesus Christ and have faith in Him because their hearts were soften and ready to accept Jesus Christ as their savior from the preaching of John the Baptist.

It was the same when John Williams first arrived in the Pacific Islands. The good news (The Gospel) John Williams brought to the Pacific Islands prepared the hearts of the people to accept the true restored gospel that has the authority of God and the fullness of the gospel of Jesus Christ that came later after John Williams.

The church of my parent that I grew up with, helps me to learned and to understood that God never change from the beginning, yesterday, today, and tomorrow. *"For I am the*

Lord, I change not; therefore ye sons of Jacob are not consumed" *(Malachi 3:6). "Jesus Christ the same yesterday, and today and forever" (Hebrews 13:8).* From the beginning, God always speaks through His servants the prophets *"Surely the Lord God will do nothing, but revealeth his secret unto his servants the prophet"* (Amos 3:7). The Lord always speaks through His living prophets.

Now, with the restored gospel of Jesus Christ on the earth, we can learn the truth about, *"Where we came from, Why we are here on earth and Where we're going after this life,"* especially the plan of salvation and the great atonement that God's only Begotten Son Jesus Christ has sacrificed for all His children to be able to return to His presence in eternity.

The true purpose of this life is to learn as much as we can. The true learning purpose of our existence, Elder David A Bednar said, *"You and I are here on earth to prepare for eternity, to learn how to learn, to learn the things that are temporally important and eternally essential, and to assist others to learning wisdom and truth" (see Doctrine & Covenants 97:1) "Understanding who we are, where we came from, why we are on earth place upon each of us a great responsibility to learn how to learn and to learn to love learning" (Increase in Learning by David A Bednar).*

The overarching purpose of Heavenly Father's great plan of happiness is to provide His spirit children with opportunities to learn. The Atonement of Jesus Christ and the agency afforded to all of the Father's children through the redeemer's infinity and eternal sacrifice are divinely designed to facilitate our learning. The Savior said, *"Learn of me and listen to my words: and walk in the meekness of my spirit, and you shall have peace in me" (Doctrine & Covenants 19:23).*

After we experienced our spiritual birth, Heavenly Father counseled and corrected us and we were instructed, enlightened, and edified in His holy presence. Now that we have experienced our physical birth in mortality, He desires to continue to communicate with us and to give us counsel and direction. He does this through personal revelation, which involves preparation, prayers and promptings.

Personal revelation is one of the greatest gift and blessings we can receive. Personal revelation is a communication from God to His children. We can learn direct from God through personal revelation by the Holy Ghost and the gift of the Holy Ghost, reading, scripture studying, following the teaching of the living prophets, and asking the Lord in prayers. Our Father in Heaven is willing to teach us and communicate with us, but sometimes our hearts are not been able to receive these personal revelations to learn and to gain understanding. Our hearts need to be soften, prepared to receive, have the desire to know, and be worthy.

The Apostle Peter knew of a surety that Jesus was the Christ, the Son of the living God. The Savior explained that the source for Peter's knowledge was not flesh and blood, but the Father which is in Heaven. As we come unto Christ, we can feel and know of surety, not with our hands or eyes but with all our heart and mind that Jesus is the Christ.

We repeatedly are admonished in revelations to ask in faith when we lack of knowledge (James 1:5-6). "To seek learning, even by study and also by faith" (Doctrine & Covenants 88:118). "And to inquire of God that we might receive instructions from his spirit" (Doctrine & Covenants 6:14). "And know mysteries which are great and marvelous" (Doctrine & Covenants 6:11). The restored church of Jesus Christ exists to help individuals and families learn about and receive the blessings of the Savior's gospel.

President Brigham Young (1801-1877) was a learner. It's marvelous both the way he learned and how much he learned. He never ceases learning from the revelation of the Lord, from the scriptures and from good books. He clearly learned to love learning. He ultimately became a powerful disciple and teacher precisely because he first was an effective learner. President Young repeatedly taught that "*The object of (our mortal) existence is to learn"* The following statements by President Young emphasize this truth.

The religion embraced by the Latter-day Saint, if only slightly understood, prompts them to search diligently after knowledge. "*There are no other people in existence more eager to see, hear, learn and understand truth. Put forth your ability to learn as fast as you can and gather all the strength of mind, and principal of faith, you possibly can and then distribute your knowledge to the people."*

"*We are in school (of mortality) and keep learning and we do not expect to cease learning while we live on the earth, and when we pass through the veil, we expect still to continue to* learn and increase our fund of information. That may appear some strange idea to some, but it is for a plain and simple reason that we are not capacitated to receive all knowledge at once. We must therefore receive a little here and a little there."

The prophet Abinadi explain the role of the feeling that comes from God to our hearts. He taught that, *"We cannot understand the scriptures completely unless we apply our hearts to understanding."*

We might ask, *"when shall we cease to learn? I will give you my opinion about it, never, never."* Quote from Brigham Young.

The restored gospel of Jesus Christ or the Church of Jesus Christ of Latter -day Saints is the kingdom of God on earth has all the answers of spiritual things of God. In order for us to understand the things of God, we need His spirit to teach us and to be able to understand it. We are assisted in learning of and listening to the words of Christ by the Holy Ghost, even the third member of the Godhead.

The Holy Ghost is a true and trustworthy teacher, *"reveals and witnesses the truth of all things, teach you all things, and bring all things to your remembrance" (John 14:26, Moroni 10:5, Doctrine and Covenants 39:6).* The Holy Ghost is the teacher who kindles within us and abiding love of and for learning. And *"teach you the peaceable things of the kingdom" (Doctrine & Covenants 36:2).* The Holy Ghost is a revelator. Joseph Smith said, no man can receive the Holy Ghost without receiving revelation.

But that is not all. To one who thought that revelation would flow without effort, the Lord said: *"You have not understood; you have supposed that I would give it unto you, when you took no thought save it was to ask me. But behold, I say it unto you that you must study it out in your mind; then you must ask me if it be right, and if it is right I will cause that your bosom shall within you; you shall feel it that it is right"* (Doctrine and Covenants 9:7-8).

The burning in the bosom is not a purely physical sensation. It is more like a warm light shinning in your being. The Holy Ghost speaks with a voice that feels more than you hear. It is described as a *"still small voice."* And while we speak of *"listening"* to the whisperings of the spirit, most often one described a spiritual prompting by saying, *"I had a feeling."* Revelations comes as words we feel more than we hear.

The scriptures are full of expressions as *"The veil was taken from our mind, the eyes of our understanding were opened,"* or *"I will tell you in your mind and in your heart,"* or *"I did enlighten thy mind,"* or *"Speak the thoughts that I will put in your heart"* (Doctrine and Covenants 110:1, 6:15, 8:2, 68:4). There are hundreds of verses that teach revelation.

When we learned the purpose of been born to mortality, and why we are here, and to learned who we are, we *"CREATED,"*

CHAPTER 4

WHEN WE LEARN, WE CREATED.

When we were born to the earth, we do not remember anything from where we use to live before, because of the veil that blocked our mind and memory to remember where we came from, why we are here and how to find our way back to where we came from or where we are going after this life. In other words, the eyes of our understanding are not yet open.

With the Holy Ghost the third member of the Godhead, is the greatest gift of our Heavenly Father for all His children who has a willing heart and a desire to learn and to understand the plan of salvation.

In the beginning *"So God created man in his own image, in the image of God created he him; male and female created he them" (Genesis 1:27)*. One of the main purposes of coming to earth, our Father in Heaven wanted us to become like Him, not only in His image but perfect as He is. *"Be ye therefore perfect, even as your Father which is in heaven is perfect" (Matthew 5:48)*. *"Therefore I would that ye should be perfect even as I, or your Father which who is in heaven is perfect" (3 Nephi 12:48).* As we lived, we learned, when we learned, we can create ourselves to the image that God wants us to be in order to be worthy and to be able to be like Him when we meet Him.

Baptism Essential

To create ourselves to His perfect image or to prepare ourselves to be like Him, we need to become a member of the kingdom of God here on earth or the restored gospel of Jesus Christ. When we learned about the church that Jesus Christ and His apostles (disciples) organized when they were on the earth, it was taken away from the earth after they were all killed, now it's been restored back to the earth and it's the restored gospel of Jesus Christ, "The Church of Jesus Christ of Latter-day Saints." The Church of Jesus Christ of Latter-day Saints is the only church on the earth that has the fullness of the gospel Jesus Christ and has the saving ordinances that will enable us to return back to our God.

To become a member of this restored gospel, first we have to have faith in the Lord Jesus Christ, which is the first principal of the gospel. Second repentances which is the second principal of the gospel. Third baptism by immersion for the remission of sins. Fourth the laying on of hands, for the gift of the Holy Ghost.

Faith in the Lord Jesus Christ and repentance prepare us for the ordinances of baptism and confirmation. Jesus taught that we must be baptized by immersion of the remission, or forgiveness, of our sins. Baptism is an essential ordinance of salvation. No person can enter the Kingdom of God without been baptized. *"Except a man is born of the water and of the spirit, he cannot enter into the kingdom of God" (John 3:5).* Christ set the example for us by been baptized. *"Jesus came and was baptized of John" (Mark 1:9).*

Baptism by immersion is a symbol of the death, burial, and resurrection of the Savior. In a similar way, it represents the end of our old life of sin and a commitment to live a new life as a disciple of Christ. The Savior taught that baptism is a rebirth. When we are baptized we begin the process of being born again and become spiritual sons and daughters of Christ (Mosiah 5:7-8; Romans 8:14-17).

We must be baptized to become members of the restored church, The Church of Jesus Christ of Latter-day Saints, and to eventually enter into the Kingdom of Heaven. This ordinance is a law of God and must be performed by His authority. A bishop or mission president must give a priesthood holder permission to perform a baptism or confirmation.

"Little children do not need to be baptized and are redeemed through the mercy of Jesus Christ" (see Moroni 8:4-24). "They are not to be baptized until they reach the age of an accountability, which is eight years of age" (Doctrine & Covenants 68:27).

Baptism is a sacred ordinance for the remission or forgiveness of sins but also sacred ceremony or rite that shows that we have entered into a covenant with God. God has always required His children to make covenants. A covenant is abiding and solemn agreement between God and man. God promises to bless us, and we promise to obey Him. Keeping covenants brings blessings in this life and exaltation in the life to come. Covenants place us under a strong obligation to honor our commitments to God. To keep our covenants, we must give up activities or interests that prevent us from honoring those covenants.

For example, we give up shopping and recreational pursuits on Sunday so we can keep the Sabbath Day holy. Our covenants remind us to repent everyday of our lives. By keeping the commandments and serving others we received and retained a remission of our sins.

Covenants are usually made by means of sacred ordinances, such as baptism. These ordinances are administered by priesthood authority. Through the ordinance of baptism, for example, we covenant to take upon ourselves the name of Jesus Christ, always remember Him and keep His commandments.

As we keep our part of the covenant, God promises the constant companionship of the Holy Ghost, a remission of our sins, and being born again. Through sacred ordinances, such as baptism and confirmation, we learn about and experience God's power. (see Doctrine & Covenants)

Every Sunday we renew this baptismal covenant we made with the Lord by partaking of the sacrament. *For behold, I say unto you, that it mattereth not ye shall eat or what ye shall drink when ye partake of the sacrament, if it is so be that ye do*

*it with an eye single to my glory, remembering unto the father
my body which was laid down for you, and my blood which was
shed for the remission of your sins" (Doctrine & Covenants 27:2).*

The Gift of the Holy Ghost

Jesus taught that we must be baptized of water and also of
the spirit. Baptism by water must followed by baptism of the
spirit or it is incomplete. Only when we receive baptism and
the gift of the Holy Ghost can we receive a remission of our
sins and become completely spiritual reborn. We then begin
a new spiritual life as Disciples of Christ.

After a person is baptized by water, one or more authorized
priesthood holders lay their hands upon the person's head
and confirm the person a member of the Church of Jesus
Christ of Latter-day Saints. They then confer the gift of
Holy Ghost.

Those who receive the gift of the Holy Ghost and remain
worthy can enjoy His companionship throughout their lives.
The Holy Ghost has a sanctifying, cleansing effect upon us.
The Holy Ghost testifies of Christ and helps us recognize
the truth. He provides spiritual strength and helps us to do
what is right. He comforts us during the time of trial or
sorrow. He warns us spiritual and physical danger. The Holy
Ghost provides the power by which we teach and learn. The
gift of the Holy Ghost is one of our Heavenly Father's most
precious gifts. Through the power of the Holy Ghost we can
feel God's love and direction for us. The gift is a foretaste of
eternal joy and promise of eternal life.

The Priesthood authority need to perform this ordinance, which was lost centuries ago through apostasy, was restored through the Prophet Joseph Smith. Only through membership in the church can one receive the gift of the Holy Ghost. This authority makes the church different from any other religion in the world. By the Lord's own declaration, it is *"the only true and living church upon the face of the earth" (Doctrine & Covenants 1:30).* Having the continued guidance of the Holy Ghost is one of the benefits of being baptized and confirmed.

Endure to the End

Once we have entered the straight and narrow path by our faith in Jesus Christ, repentance, and the ordinances of baptism and confirmation, we must exert every effort to stay on the path. We do so by continually exercising faith in Jesus Christ, repenting, making commitments, and following the spirit. Once we have been forgiven of our sins, we should try every day to remain free from sin so that we can always have the Holy Ghost with us. In the covenant of baptism, we promise our Father in Heaven that we will obey His commandments for the rest of our lives. If we fall short, we must repent in order to retain the blessings of the covenant. We promise to do good works, serve others, and follow the Savior's example. In the scriptures this lifelong commitment is often called *"enduring to the end."*

By following the gospel path, we can draw closer to God, conquer temptation and sin, and enjoy the gift of the Holy Ghost more abundantly. As we patiently, faithfully, and consistently follow this path throughout our lives, we will qualify for Eternal Life and *creating* ourselves to be like our Father in Heaven.

Faith in Christ, repentance, making, renewing, and keeping covenants, and been cleansed by the spirit become a pattern of living. Our action in daily life are shaped and governed by these principal. Peace and joy come by following this way, and we gradually grow in Christ like attributes. Eventually, as we follow this way and press forward with steadfastness in Christ and endure to the end, we are promised, *"Ye shall have eternal life"* (*2 Nephi 31:20*).

All men who live worthily are to ordain to the Melchizedek Priesthood in order to receive the Temple ordinances. Some ordinances are essential to our exaltation. These ordinances are called saving ordinances. They include baptism, confirmation, ordination to the Melchizedek Priesthood (for men), the temple endowment, and the marriage sealing. With each of these ordinances, we enter into the solemn covenants with the Lord. The Temple endowment and the Marriage sealing are to be done in the Temple.

Ordinances and covenants help us remember who we are. They remind us of our duty to God. The Lord has provided them to help us come unto Him and receive eternal life. When we honor them, He strengthens us spiritually. And when we endure to end, we are *"CREATING"* ourselves to God's image and to become like him.

CHAPTER 5

WHEN WE LIVED LEARNED CREATED, WE RELATED

We can live forever with our families after this life. Our Heavenly Father's plan of happiness is for us to come to earth and to be tested and receive all the blessings and the ordinances of the restored gospel and endure to be able to return and live with Him in His presence and have Eternal Life which is His greatest gift. *"For behold this is my work and my glory to bring to pass the immortality and eternal life of man" (Moses 1:39).*

We find that we are related to God our Heavenly Father in many different ways. He is not only our Ruler and Creator; He is also our Heavenly Father. He created us in His image and He is the Father of our spirit. All men and women are sons and daughters of God. *"Man, as a spirit, was begotten and born of Heavenly parents, and reared to maturity in the eternal mansions of the Father, prior to coming upon the earth in a temporal [physical] body"* (Teaching of the Presidents of the Church: Joseph F. Smith [1998],335).

Every person who was ever born on earth is our spirit brother or sister. Because we are the spirit children of God, we have inherited the potential to develop His divine qualities. Through the Atonement of Jesus Christ, we can become like our Heavenly Father and receive a fullness of Joy.

Our Heavenly Father knew we could not progress beyond a certain point unless we left Him for a time. He wanted us to develop the God like qualities that He has. To do this we need to leave our premortal home to be tested and to gain experience. Our spirit needed to be clothed with physical bodies at death and reunite with them in resurrection. Then we would receive immortal bodies like that of our Heavenly Father. If we passed our tests we would receive the fullness of joy that our Heavenly Father has received. (Doctrine & Covenants 93: 30-34).

We can relate to our Father in Heavenly by raising our families the way the Lord has set it up in the restored gospel of Jesus Christ. One of the most important patterns to His plan is families to be seal for time and all eternity. A man and woman can enter into the new and everlasting covenant which is to be married for time and all eternity in the holy Temples of the Lord by the authority of the priesthood. (The Family A Proclamation to the World).

Before we experience our physical birth in mortality, we were spiritually born in immortality as spirit children of our Heavenly Father. He counseled and corrected us; we were instructed, enlightened and edified in His Holy Presence as a family. We belong to a most sacred family of a true living

God that has loved us more than any other love that we can think of. He wanted us to continue to live the same way in order to prepare us to live with Him after this life. Knowing God is so important that the Savior said, *"This is life eternal that they might know thee the only true God, and Jesus Christ, whom thou hast sent" (John 17:3).*

The first and the great commandment is *"Thou shalt love the Lord thy God with all thy heart, and with all thy soul, and with all thy mind" (Matthew 22:37).* The more we know God, the more we love Him and keep His commandments (see 1 John 2:3-5). By keeping His commandments we can become like Him.

We can know God if we will,

1. *Believe that he exists and that He loves us (see Mosiah 4:9).*
2. *Study the scripture (see 2 Timothy 3:14-17).*
3. *Pray to Him (see James 1:5).*
4. *Obey all His commandments as best as we can (see John 14:21-23).*

As we do these things we will come to know God and eventually have eternal life. We will learn that He is the Father of our spirit and we are His spirit sons and daughters, and we are *Related* to Him. When we lived with our Heavenly Father, He explained a plan for our progression. We could become like Him, an exalted being. The plan required that we be separated from Him and come to earth. This separation was necessary to prove whether we would obey our Father's commandments even though we were no longer in His presence. The plan provided that when earth life ended, we would be judged and rewarded according to the degree of our faith and obedience.

Exaltation is Eternal Life, the kind of life God lives. He lives in great glory. He is perfect. He possesses all knowledge and all wisdom. He is the Father of spirit children. He is a creator. We can become like our Heavenly Father. This is exaltation.

If we prove faithful to the Lord, we will live in the highest degree of the Kingdom of Heaven. We will become exalted, to live with our Heavenly Father in eternal families. Exaltation is the greatest gift that Heavenly Father can give His children (see *Doctrine & Covenants 14:7*).

Our Heavenly Father is perfect, and He glories in the fact that it is possible for His children to become like him. His work and glory is "*To bring to pass the immortality and eternal life of man*" *(Moses 1:39)*.

Those who receive exaltation in the celestial kingdom through faith in Jesus Christ will receive special blessings the Lord has promised, "*All things are theirs*" *(Doctrine & Covenants 132:19-20)*. These are some of the blessings given to exalted people:

1. *They will live eternally in the presence of Heavenly Father and Jesus Christ (Doctrine & Covenants 76:62).*

2. *They will become gods (Doctrine & Covenants 132:20-23).*

3. *They will be united eternally with their righteous family members and will be able to have eternal increase.*

4. *They will receive a fullness of Joy.*

5. *They will have everything that our Heavenly Father and Jesus Christ have—all power, glory, dominion, and knowledge (Doctrine & Covenants 132:19-20*

Presidents Joseph Fielding Smith wrote: "*The Father has promised through the son that all that he has shall be given to those who are obedient to His commandments. They shall increase in knowledge, wisdom, and power, going from grace to grace, until the fullness of the perfect day shall burst upon them*" (Doctrine of Salvation, comp. Bruce R. McConkie, 3 vols. [1954-56], 2:36; italics in original).

The Lord has said, "*If you keep my commandments and endure to the end you shall have eternal life, which gift is the greatest of all the gifts of God*" (Doctrine & Covenants 14:7). President Joseph Fielding Smith said, "*If we will continue in God; that is, keep his commandments, worship him and live his truth; then the time will come when we shall be bathed in the fullness of truth which shall grow brighter and brighter until the perfect day*" (Doctrine of Salvation, 2:36)

The Prophet Joseph Smith taught; "*When you climb up a ladder, you must begin at the bottom, and ascend step by step, until you arrive at the top; and so it is with the principal of the gospel—you must begin with the first, and go on until you learn all the principal of exaltation. But it will be great while after you have passed through the veil [died] before you will have learned them. It is not all to be comprehended in this world; it will be great work to learn our salvation and exaltation even beyond the grave" (Teaching of President of the Church: Joseph Smith [2007], 268).*

Joseph Smith taught: *"It is the first principle of the gospel to know for a certainty the Character of God ... He was once a man like us; God himself, the Father of us all, dwelt on an earth, the same as Jesus Christ himself did" (Teaching of the Prophet Joseph Smith, sel. Joseph Fielding Smith [1976], 345-46).*

Our Heavenly Father knows our trials, our weaknesses, and our sins. He has compassion and mercy on us. He wants us to succeed even as He did. Imagine what joy each of us will have when we return to our Heavenly Father if we can say: *"Father I lived according to thy will. I have been faithful and have kept Thy commandments. I am happy to be home again."* Then we will hear Him say, *"Well done ... thou hast been faithful over a few things, I will make thee ruler over many things: enter thou into the joy of thy Lord" (Matthew 25:23).d*

That is the whole purpose of the plan of salvation. We came from the premortal life where we lived with our Heavenly Father before we were born to earth. We lived as spirit children of God, and there we received the plan that we would be able to follow when we come to earth. That's where we came from. When we were born to mortality (earth life) we are to receive the body of flesh and bones and to be tested if we would obey Him and be able to return back to Him and live with Him again. And that is why we are here on the earth.

When it comes to the end of this earthly life, it is very important how we endure until death, because it will reward us in the next life after death. Through the Atonement of Jesus Christ, all people will be resurrected. After we will be resurrected, we will stand before the Lord to be judged according to our desires and actions. Each of us will accordingly receive an eternal dwelling place a specific kingdom of glory. The Lord taught this principal when He said, *"In my father's house have many mansions" (John 14:2).*

There are three kingdom of glory: the Celestial kingdom, the Terrestrial kingdom, and the Telestial kingdom. The glory we will inherit will depend on the depth of our conversion, expressed by our obedience to the Lord's commandments. It will depend on the manner in which we have *"received the testimony of Jesus" (Doctrine & Covenants 76:51 see also 76:74, 79, & 101).*

The Celestial Kingdom is the highest of the three kingdoms of glory. Those in this kingdom will dwell forever in the presence of God the Father and His Son Jesus Christ. This should be your goal: to inherit the Celestial glory and to help others receive that great blessing as well. Such a goal is not achieved in one attempt; it is a result of a lifetime of righteousness and constancy of purpose.

The Celestial Kingdom is a place prepared for those who have *"received the testimony of Jesus Christ"* and been *"made perfect through Jesus the mediator of the new covenant, who wrought out this perfect atonement through the shedding of his own blood" (Doctrine & Covenants 76:51, 69)*. To inherit this gift, we must receive the ordinances of salvation, keep the commandment, and repent of our sins.

The diagram below will give you a clear picture of what the plan of salvation is talking about step by step. When you study and learn it from the scripture it will give you a sure understanding that God has a great wise plan for His children to learn and to become like Him and to be worthy to return and live with Him again.

It also open up the eyes of our understanding that was blocked from the veil to know where we come from, why we're here on earth, and where we're going after this life. The plan of salvations was presented to us in the pre-existence. But the restored gospel of Jesus Christ or the Church of Jesus Christ of Latter-day Saints is the only church that has the fullness of the gospel of Jesus Christ that understands this plan.

When we were borned in mortality we LIVED. When we LIVED we LEARNED. When we LEARNED we CREATED. When we CREATED we RELATED.

CHAPTER 6

PLAN OF SALVATION

Our Eternal Life

Many of us spent our lives looking for something to hold on to, something that will last. We look for ways to avoid aging or become famous or rich. But we eventually realized that mortal life is temporary. Friends and family members grow old and die, the famous are soon forgotten, and wealth is lost as quickly as it won.

Our hope and happiness lie in knowing who we are, where we came from, and where we can go. We are children of eternal God. Our lives can be compare to a three – act play: premortal life (before we came to earth), mortal life (our time here on earth), and post mortal life (where we go after this life). God has had a plan for our life since the beginning of the first act-a plan that, if followed, provides comfort and guidance now, as well as salvation and eternal happiness in our post mortal life.

Understanding the following can help us live a happier life now and in eternity. We are eternal beings. We lived as spirits before we were born and we will continue to live after we die.

- **Pre-Earth Life: God's Purpose and Plan for Us**
  - God is our Heavenly Father, and we are His children (see Acts 17:16-34; Hebrews 12:9).
  - God has a plan for our happiness. Jesus Christ is central to that plan.
  - God's plan of happiness makes it possible to return to his presence (see Moses 1:39).
  - Our eternal progression depends on how we use our agency (see 2Nephi 2:27-29).

- **The Creation**
  - - Under the Father's direction, Jesus Christ created the earth (Hebrews 1:1-3).

- **Agency and the Fall of Adam and Eve**
  - Adam and Eve were created in God's Image (see Genesis 1:26-27).
  - In the Garden of Eden they were innocent and lived in God's presence.
  - Because they partook of the forbidden fruit, they were cast out of the garden (see Moses 4:19-31). This is called the fall.
  - They became mortal, were able to have children, and were also subject to sin and death (see 2 Nephi 2:22-25; Moses 5:11).

- **Our Life on Earth**
  - Our purpose in life is to find lasting peace, joy, and happiness as families and to prepare to return to live with God.
  - We came to the earth to be tested (see Abraham 3:24-25).
  - We gain a body of a flesh and bones, but we are subject to physical death.
  - God gives commandments. If we obey, we are blessed. If we disobey, we sin and receive the consequences.
  - All sin must be paid for, either by ourselves or by Christ (see Doctrine & Covenants 19:15-20).
  - We make choices, and we all commit sin (see Romans 3:23
  - We have experiences that bring us happiness and also sorrow.
  - We cannot overcome either physical or spiritual death without Christ.

- **The Atonement**
  - Because Jesus Christ overcame physical death, we will all be resurrected (Alma 11:41- 43).
  - Through Christ's Atonement we can become clean from sin so we can become clean from sin so that we can return to live in God's presence (see 2 Nephi 9:8-9).
  - Christ will forgive our sin as we have faith in him, repent, receive baptism and the gift of the Holy Ghost, and endure to the end.

- **The Spirit World**
  - All people must die.
  - At death our spirits go to the spirit world.
  - We live in either a state of misery or a state of peace and rest, depending on how we lived in this life

- **The resurrection, Judgment, and Immortality**
  - Our spirits and bodies will be reunited in the resurrection (see Alma 11: 42-45; 40:23).
  - We will return to God's presence to be Judged according to our works and desires.
  - If we have repented, we will receive mercy
  - Eternal life is a gift of God given to those who fully obey the gospel of Jesus Christ (see Doctrine & Covenants 14:7).

- **Kingdoms of Glory** (see **Doctrine & Covenants 76; 137; 1 Corinthians** 15:40-42)
  - We receive rewards according to our works and desires (see Doctrine & Covenants 137:9).
  - Those who receive the gospel and live it valiantly throughout their lives will receive the **celestial kingdom** (see Doctrine & Covenants 76:50-70).
  - Honorable people who are "blinded by the craftiness of men" and who are "not valiant in the testimony of Jesus [Christ]" receive the **terrestrial kingdom** (see Doctrine & Covenants 76:75, 79).

- Those who sin and do not repent will receive the **telestial glory** after they suffer and pay for their sins.

God Is Our Father
God is the Father of our spirits (Hebrews 12:9). We are created in his image. (Genesis 1:26) We have a divine nature and destiny.

We Live With God
Before we were born, we lived with God, the father of our spirits. (Hebrews 12:9) All persons on earth are literally brothers and sisters in the family of God.

Earth Life Is Part of God's Plan
Our life on earth has purpose. Coming to earth is part of God plan for us to gain physical body and learn to choose between good and evil. (Abraham 3:24-25)

Jesus Christ Is the Way
Our Heavenly Father sent his son, Jesus Christ, to be our Savior and show us the way to live according to God's plan. (John 14:6)

We Can Find Happiness
Following God's plan for us is the surest way to find happiness and endure life's challenges. (James 5:11)

We Can Live with God Again
Our lives will not end when we die. Our future lives are determined by the way we live our lives now. (Ecclesiastes 12:7)

God's Plan Of Salvation

"For as in Adam all die, even so in Christ all made alive" (1 Corinthians 15:22).

Where did I come from and why?

It's hard to move forward when you don't know where you're headed and why. God's plan gives us the answers to life's most basic questions like, *"Where did I come from? What's my purpose here? And, what happens when I die?"* Knowing the answers gives us hope and helps us find peace and joy.

Our life didn't begin at birth and it won't end at death. Before we came to earth, our spirits lived with God, who created us. We knew Him, and He knew and loved us. It was a happy time during which we were taught God's plan of happiness and the path of true joy. But just as most of us leave our home and parents when we grow up, God knew we need to do the same. He knew we couldn't progress unless we left for awhile. So He allows us to come to the earth to experience the joy as well as the pain of a physical body.

One thing that makes this life so hard sometimes is that we are out of God's physical presence. Not only that, but we cannot remember our pre-earth life which means we have to operate by faith rather than sight. God did not say it would be easy, but promised His Spirit would be there when we needed Him. Even though it feels like it sometimes, we are not alone in our journey.

God's plan for us is beautiful and simple. He wants us to have joy and to become like Him.

That doesn't mean He expect us to be perfect. He knows you won't be. But He does expect that while you're here on earth you try to the best of your ability to be more like Him and that you learn and grow from your mistakes. Each time you make a poor choice with painful consequences, that decision lead to unhappiness—sometimes immediately, sometimes much later. Likewise, choosing good eventually leads to happiness and help you become more like Heavenly Father.

Just as God created the earth as a place for us to live and gain experience, He created us. And He gave us a body of a flesh and blood in the likeness of His gloried body. In the Old Testament God said, "*Let us make men in our own image, after our likeness" (Genesis 1:26*). Jacob had declared that he had seen God "*Face to Face" (Genesis 32:30).* Moses also spoke with God "*Face to Face, as man speakth unto his friend" (Exodus 33:11).* In the New Testament, when the resurrected Christ appeared to His Apostles, He told them, "*Handle me and see; for a spirit hath not a flesh and bones, as ye see me have" (Luke 24:39).*

ADAM AND EVE GAVE US THE GIFT OF CHOICE

You may know the story of Adam and Eve in the Garden of Eden, but did you know they paved the way for the rest of us to come to earth, make choices, and become like our Heavenly Father?

59

As God's first children on the earth, Adam and Eve were living in their garden paradise. They didn't feel any sorrow or pain, which might seems nice, except that without it, they also couldn't feel joy. They didn't remember their pre-earth life. If they hadn't eaten the forbidden fruit, they would have lived like that forever and never had children. Mankind never would have been born or populated.

As we know, Adam and Eve succumbed to Satan's Temptation to eat the fruit and disobeyed God who had commanded them not to eat from the tree of knowledge of good and evil. As a consequence, they were separated from God's presence physically and spiritually—an event we refer to as the fall. They became mortal—just as we are—subject to sin, disease, all types of suffering, and ultimately death. But it wasn't all bad because they could now feel great joy. *"Adam fell that men might be; and men are that they might have joy" (2 Nephi 2:25).*

But as they were obedient to the gospel of Jesus Christ Adam and Eve were able to receive God's inspiration, revelation, and even visits from Heavenly messengers.

Once out of the garden, they were able to progress and learn to become more like our Heavenly Father. In addition, they could have children, which mean the rest of God's spirit children (all of us) could come to earth, experience physical bodies, and be proven by our daily choices. Just like Adam and Eve, there are consequences to all our choices, good or bad. Lasting happiness and progression comes from choosing to do what God wants us to do. The key word is "*choosing.*" Generally God does not step in and prevent us from making poor choices Satan tempts us to make. He will, however, offer His love, divine guidance, and warnings when we open our heart to Him.

THE SECRET OF HAPPINESS

Regardless of what you do or don't have in this life, your deepest, most lasting happiness will come from knowing God's plan and following it.

We often fall into a trap of thinking a new car, job promotion, beauty makeover, or some level of frame will make us happy. And often they do—for a time. But it never last because wealth, power, beauty and fame simply don't bring lasting happiness, as much as they wish they would. Rather, true happiness comes from following Christ's example and developing God like attributes such as goodness, love, justice and mercy. It comes from serving others and helping them to follow the example and the teaching of Jesus Christ. It comes from overcoming the appetites of our human bodies and instead of following the prompting of the Spirit. It comes from working hard and has a healthy lifestyle, friends, family, and personal achievements. Regardless of what you do or don't have in this life, your deepest, most lasting happiness will come from knowing God's plan and following it.

When Bad Things Happen

Sometimes bad things happen even when we make good choices.

We get sick. Loved ones die. We lose our job or home. Our spouse is unfaithful. It's hard not to ask why God allows us to suffer so much. Know that while God take no pleasure in your suffering, your difficulties, regardless of their cause can bring you closer to Him and even make you stronger if you endure faithfully.

"Nevertheless, Jacob, my firstborn in the wilderness, thou knowest the greatness of God; and he shall consecrate thine afflictions for thy gain" (2 Nephi 2:2). "As many as I love, I rebuke and chasten: be zealous therefore, and repent" (Revelation 3:19).

It's comforting to know that God's Son, Jesus Christ, suffered all things. He understands your pain and can help you through your trials. When you have faith in God and His plan, you can be assured that there's a purpose to all that happens to you here on earth. Our time here is short compare to our eternal life. As the Lord told Joseph Smith during a period of intense suffering, *"Know thou, my son, that all these things shall give thee experience, and shall be for thy good. The Son of Man had descended below them all. Art thou greater than he?" (Doctrine & Covenants 122:7-8).*

Coping with calamities can strengthen us and make us more compassionate. It can help us learn, grow and to serve others. Dealing with adversity is one of the chief ways you're tested and tutored in your life here on earth. Our loving Heavenly Father has the ability to compensate us for any injustice we may be called upon to endure in this mortal life. If we endure faithfully He will rewarded us beyond our ability to comprehend in the life to come.

"But as it is written, Eye hath not seen, nor ear heard, neither have entered into the heart of man, the things which God hath prepared for them that love him" (1 Corinthian 2:9).

Amazingly with God's help you can experience joy even in times of trials, and face life's challenges with the spirit of peace.

GOD'S PLAN—WHAT JESUS CHRIST DID FOR US

Heavenly Father knew you would make mistakes in this mortal life.

Your mistake might be as simple as hurting your friend's feelings, or a sin far more serious. Seeing the pain we've caused and the feelings the misery of remorse, shame and guilt can sometimes be overwhelming and devastating. We wonder if we can overcome our mistakes and feel the peace of forgiven. We unequivocally can, because of the atonement of Jesus Christ and the process of repentance. We can confess our sin to God and ask for forgiveness. And He's promised that *"He will remember them no more" (Doctrine & Covenants 58:42).*

It works because Heavenly Father sent His Son, Jesus Christ, to voluntarily suffer and pay for our sins and sorrows by atoning for them Himself. We can't fully understand how Jesus Christ suffered for our sins. But we know that in the Garden of Gethsemane, the weight of our sins cause Him such agony that He bled from every pore (*Luke 22:39-44*). Later, as He hung upon the cross, Jesus willingly suffered painful death by one of the cruelest methods ever known (*Alma 7:11*). However, His mental and spiritual anguish went well beyond the pain of the cross. The Savior tells us,

"For behold I, God, have suffered these things for all, that they might not suffer if they would repent" (Doctrine & Covenants 19:16-17).

In addition, to ask for God's forgiveness, He also wants us to ask forgiveness of those we've harmed, see if we can repair the damage, and promise not to repeat the same mistakes. Then we can move forward feeling God's love, and the incredible peace and joy that comes from been fully forgiven.

To make His Atonement Fully Effective in Our Lives, We need to

- *Exercise Faith in Him*
- *Repent*
- *Be Baptized*
- *Receive the Holy Ghost*
- *Choose To Follow His Teaching the Rest of Our Lives*

WHAT HAPPEN WHEN WE DIE

Picture your hand inside the glove. The glove moves only when your hand does. Take your hand out and the gloves sits lifeless on the table. This is an easy way to visualize what happen when you die. Imagine your body is the glove operated by who you really are – your spirit. When we die our bodies gets left behind, lifeless like a glove, but our spirit lives forever.

Countless scriptures and personal accounts by prophets throughout time have told us this is true.

Our physical death is not the end, rather a step forward in our Heavenly Father's plan and a time of indescribable joy for the person making the transition.

When you are the one left behind—the one losing a friend or a love one—the pain of that loss is very real. But there's a lot of comfort in knowing that we'll see him or her again. And because of Christ's death, at some point our spirit and body will be reunited *(resurrected)* and made perfect never be separated again.

IMMORTALITY—One of God's Greatest Gift

If you could have one wish, what would it be?

Most of us would probably say we want to live forever. That's exactly what God gave each of us when He sent His Son, Jesus Christ, to die for us and to atone for our sins. It's called resurrection and everyone born on earth, even wicked people, will receive this gift immortality (*1Corinthian 15:21-22*).

On the 3rd day of His Crucifixion, Jesus Christ was became the first person to be resurrected. His spirit was reunited with His glorified, perfected body and He could no longer die. When Christ's friend went to visit His tomb, angel said, *"He is not here: for he is risen, as he said" (Matthew 28:6).*

"WILL I GO TO HEAVEN?"

Yes! God will judge all men fairly and reward them appropriately with a place in His Kingdom.

CHAPTER 7

WHY THE TRUTH NEED
TO BE SHARE

Many people have accepted this truth and become faithful members of the Restored Gospel of Jesus Christ or The Church of Jesus Christ of Latter-day Saints or The Kingdom of God on earth. They have learned that this is the only church on the face of the earth that has the fullness of the gospel of Jesus Christ. This same gospel was taught in the time of Jesus Christ and His Apostles when they were on the earth. The gospel was lost and the authority was taken away when Christ and His apostles got killed and the church they organized was not on the earth and now is been restored back on the earth.

As members of the restored gospel of Jesus Christ we live and learned a great deal of knowledge from God through His living prophets, personal revelations, the scriptures and the greatest teacher, the Holy Ghost with its many gifts. As we learned this truth we apply it in our lives and live it, it will brings us more closely to the knowledge of our God and His wise plan of salvation.

As we learned this truth, not only that we are preparing ourselves to return back to live with our Father in Heaven, but we have to share it to our brothers and sisters who never heard of it or have no knowledge of understanding who God is and do not understand the purpose of life here on earth and do not know how to return back to Him who sent us here to earth.

A Divine Commission

The Church of Jesus Christ of Latter-day Saints or The Restored Gospel of Jesus Christ is a missionary church. Missionary is a follower of Christ that testifies of Him as the Redeemer and proclaims the truth of His gospel. Devoted disciples of Jesus Christ always have been and always will be valiant missionaries.

The Church of Jesus Christ always has been and always will be a missionary church. The individual members of the Savior's church have accepted the solemn obligation to assist in fulfilling the divine commission given by the Lord to His Apostles, as recorded in the New Testament.

"Go ye therefore, and teach all nations, baptizing them in the name of the Father, and of the Son, and of the Holy Ghost:

"Teaching them to observe all things what so ever I have commanded you: and lo, I am with you always, even unto the end of the world. Amen" (Matthew 28:19-20).

Latter-day Saints take seriously this responsibility to teach all people in all nations about the Lord Jesus Christ and His restored gospel. We believed the same church founded by the Savior anciently has been reestablished on the earth by Him in the latter days. The doctrine, principles, priesthood authority, ordinances and the covenants of His gospel are found in His church.

When we invite you to come to church with us or learn with our full-time missionaries, we are not trying to sell you a product. As members of the church, we do not receive prizes or bonus points in a heavenly contest. We are not seeking simply to increase the numerical size of the church. And most importantly, we are not attempting to coerce you to believe as we do. We are inviting you to hear the restored truth of the gospel of Jesus Christ so you can study, ponder, pray and come to know for yourself if the things that we are sharing are true.

Some of you may respond, "*But I already believe in Jesus and follow his teaching …* or "*I am not sure if God really exist.*" Our invitations to you are not an attempt to diminish your religious tradition of life experience. Bring all that you know is true, good and praiseworthy and test our message. Just as Jesus beckoned two of His disciples "*come and see" (John 1:39).* So we urge you to come and see if the restored gospel of Jesus Christ enlarges and enriches that which you already believe to be true.

Indeed, we feel solemn responsibility to carry this message to every nation, kindred, tongue and people. And that is precisely what we are doing with a force today of more than 88,000 full-time missionaries laboring in over 150 sovereign states around the world. These remarkable men and women helps the members of our church fulfill the divinely appointed and individual responsibility each of us has to proclaim the everlasting gospel of Jesus Christ. (*Doctrine & Covenants 68:1) (Talk by Elder David A. Bednar, Come and See. October/2014 General Conference*)

More Than a Spiritual Duty

But our eagerness to declare this message is not merely the result of a sense of spiritual duty. Rather, our desire to share the restored gospel of Jesus Christ with you is the reflection of how important these truths are to us. I believe I can best describe why we are so forthright in seeking to explain our beliefs to you through sharing of one favorite missionary story when I was serving in Apia Samoa Mission.

There was a man who was well known in the village that he has the sweetest apple in the whole village. The man was very proud of himself and believes that he is the only farmer that has the sweetest apple in the whole village. One day the man was reading a news paper. All in the sudden he came to an article, there is an old man advertising his apple farm claiming he got the sweetest apple in the whole world.

The man stopped reading, first he was angry. Second he did not want to believe what he read on the paper to be true. The man think for a while and said to himself, the only way I can find out if this is true, is for me to go and see it himself. The man starts his journey to see this old man's apple farm if it is true that he got the sweetest apples in the world.

The man got to the farm, and it was all bar wired, and makes him difficult to get into the farm. He looked for some way to get into the farm, but he saw many branches of the apple trees inside of the farm hanging outside of the bar wire fence with lots of apple fruit on it. So instead of trying to get inside of the farm, the man just picked the apples that are hanging out of the fence and tasted it. As he tasted most of the apples which are hanging out from the fence, it was very sour to the taste and not sweet as it was advertised on the paper.

With the big smile on the man's face with a loud laughter saying, this is not true and I have to tell the world it's not true. When he was about to leave to return home, a loud voice came out from inside of the apple farm saying, *"Stop, climb up the fence and come inside and taste the apples inside until you reach the one in the middle of the farm."*

The man climbed up the fence and jumped inside and started tasting the apples as the voice instructed him. Every time he tasted and move toward the middle of the farm, it gets sweeter and sweeter until he gets into the middle of the farm it was sweeter than ever. With no more doubt, the man proved to himself that this old man's apple in his farm is sweeter than his.

As he was enjoying the sweetness of the apples in the middle center of the farm, the voice came again and said, you have proven to yourself that my farm has the sweetest apples in the whole world, so I now ask you to leave the farm. The man didn't want to leave the farm because of the sweetness of the apples. But because of the truth that he now proved himself, he has to share it and tells everybody. When he left the farm all he wants to do is to share and tell everybody that this old man has the sweetest apples in the whole world. He wants everybody to taste it themselves.

The Sweetness of the Gospel is in the Middle Center

The most important part of the story that he went to see and proved to himself that the old man has the sweetest apples in his apple farm. He did not believe it until he went and see it and proved it to himself by tasting it. And when the man got into the middle center of the farm, it was true that these apples are sweeter than his and he did not want to leave even he was told to leave. And when he left, all he wanted to do is to share it and tell everybody in the village that this old man's apple farm has the sweetest apples in the whole village.

When the man first arrived at the apple farm, he first tasted the apples that are hanging outside of the fence. These are the sour apples that anyone can partake of and leave because they are not sweet. It is the same with learning the restored gospel of Jesus Christ. Many have the opportunity to come and learn and see it for themselves or invited to attend church with us, but they did not want to know the truth, they didn't want give up activities or interest that are against the commandments of God and they love the lust of the world more than God.

Some sour apples are those who joined the church and do not keep the commandments and covenants they make with God, they don't study, they don't learn and live the gospel, and when trials comes they become offended and cannot deal with it, than they leave the church or they live wickedly. But for those who join the church and become true followers of Christ and live the fullness of the gospel to the end, they have tasted the sweetness of the gospel and never be immoveable to the end. Sour apples are likely to those members who does not rooted themselves deep down to the foundation or build upon the rock Jesus Christ was talking about. *(Matthew 7:24-27)* Sour apples are those stopped coming to church because they don't like the leaders or other members of the church, or complaining about something or easily been offended.

What is important in the story is when he reaches the middle center of the apple farm, the voice came asking him to leave but he didn't want to leave because of the sweetness of the apples in the middle center. And when he left the farm all he wanted to do is to share the story of the experience to everyone that this apple farm has the sweetest apple in the village.

When he first read the article in the news paper, he didn't want to believe it. Secondly he was angry and he didn't want to know it's true. Even though that he didn't want this to be true, but the only way that he can find out the truth, is for him to go and see and find out himself.

The sweetest apples that are found in the middle center of the farm is liken unto the deep doctrines and principles of the restored gospel of Jesus Christ. When we become members of the restored gospel of Jesus Christ, we give all ourselves to learning, give service, obedience, and enduring, you will taste the spiritual sweetness of the restored gospel of Jesus Christ and nothing will make you leave or chase you out from been a member of the restored gospel of Jesus Christ. The sweetness is the knowledge and the wisdom in the restored gospel of Jesus Christ. And when we have that knowledge and wisdom of the gospel, it enlightens up our whole selves and gives us truth. And when that truth stays within us, all we want to do is to share it, and inviting people to come and see it because that was the spirit of God who bears witness of the truth.

"Even the Spirit of truth; whom the world cannot receive, because it seeth him not, neither knoweth him: but ye know him; for he dwelleth with you, and shall be in you" (John 14:17). "But when the Comforter is come, whom I will send unto you from the Father, even the Spirit of truth, which proceedeth from the Father, he shall testify of me" (John 15:26).

When he gave the opportunity to go and see, not only that he found out the truth but he learned and prove it to himself that it is true. And when he found out that it was true, he immediately wanted to tell and share to the people of the village the truth that this old man has the sweetest apples in the whole world. The man didn't have to be urged, challenged, prompted or goaded to act. His desire to share is the natural consequence of most learning experiences and beneficial personal experience.

Many of us adults behave in precisely the same way when we humble ourselves and give a chance to go and see to prove it to ourselves anything if it is true by receiving counsel that enable us to face challenges with courage and perplexities with patience. Sharing with other people things that are most meaningful or have helped us is not unusual at all.

This same pattern is especially evident in matters of great spiritual importance and consequence. For example, an account in volume of scriptures known as the Book of Mormon highlights dream received by an ancient prophet-leader named Lehi. The central features in Lehi's dream is the tree of life-which is a representation of *"the love of God …* that is *"most desirable above all things …* and *"most joyous to the soul"* (*1 Nephi 11:22-23; see also 1Nephi 8:12, 15*).

Lehi Explain:

"It came to pass that I did go forth and partake of the fruit thereof; and I beheld that it was most sweet, above all that I ever tasted. Yea, I beheld that the fruit thereof was white, to exceed all the whiteness that I had ever seen … "And as I partook of the fruit thereof it filled my soul with exceedingly great joy; wherefore, I began to be desirous that my family should partake of it also; for I knew that it was desirable above all other fruit" (1Nephi 8:11-12).

The greatest manifestation of God's love for His children is the mortal ministry, atoning sacrifice, and the resurrection of the Lord Jesus Christ. The fruit of the tree can be considered a symbol for the blessings of the Savior's Atonement. Lehi's instant response to partaking of the fruit of the tree and experiencing great joy was an increased desire to share with and serve his family. Thus, as he turned to Christ, he also turned outward in love and service.

The enduring lesson that we learned from these two episodes is the important of experiencing in our personal lives the blessings of the atonement of Jesus Christ as a prerequisite to heartfelt and authentic service stretches far beyond merely *"going through the motion."* Much like Lehi and the old man's sweetest apples in his farm story, I recounted we as member of The Church of Jesus Christ of Latter-day Saints have felt the anguish associated with uncertainty and sin. We also have experienced the cleansing, the peace of conscience, the spiritual healing and renewal, and the guidance that are obtained only by learning and living the principle of the Savior's gospel.

The atonement of Jesus Christ provides the cleanser necessary to made pure and clean, the soothing salve to heal spiritual wounds and remove guilds, and the protections that enable us to be faithful in times both good and bad.

Absolute Truth Exists

To you family members and friends who are not members of the Church of Jesus Christ of Latter-day Saints, I have attempted to explained fundamental reasons why we are missionaries.

Absolute truth exists in a world that increasingly disdains and dismisses absolutes. In a future day, *"Every knee shall bow"* and *"every tongue shall confess that Jesus is Lord, to the glory of God the Father" (Philippians 2:10-11).* Jesus the Christ is the absolutely is the only Begotten Son of the Eternal Father. As members of His Church, we witness He lives and His church has been restored in its fullness in these latter days.

The invitation that we extend to you to learn about and test our message grow out of the positive effects the gospel of Jesus Christ has had in our lives. Sometimes we may be awkward or even relentless in our attempts. Our simple desire is to share with you the truths that are greatest worth to us.

Summary

To ask yourself *"Where do we come from? Why are we here? Where are we going from here?"* Many have reached higher goals of accomplishment in education, wealth of the world, great talent and many others success opportunities have made them happy in this life and enjoyed it until death come.

To most of us when death comes, that is the end of everything. I have witnessed most of our brothers and sisters who married in the law of the land, have end everything they planned and hoped for when death comes. They slowly change into a new start of life and slowly forgotten the first marriage life.

"If in this life only we have hope in Christ, we are of all men most miserable"(1 Corinthians 15:19). We should have hope in Christ in this life and eternal life. Our birth is not the beginning of our life and death is not the end of our life. The Lord Jesus Christ was borned as a child and was crucified and died and was resurrected on the third day and now He lived with the Father forever. *"For behold, this is my work and my glory to bring to pass the immortality and eternal life of man" (Moses 1:39).*

Many have talked about families can be forever but they don't even know they need to have knowledge and understanding of how can it be done to be seal for time and all eternity. There is a process in order for families to be forever or to live continually for time and all eternity. *"Verily I say unto you, whatsoever ye shall bind on earth shall be bound in heaven: and whatsoever ye shall loose on earth shall be loosed in heaven" (Matthew 18:18).*

Many have lost and miss their great relationships with their love ones because of death. Some they don't know where to find how families can be forever or don't even care what happen at all. Many they don't even want to know or even want to learn because they don't want to change their belief but they love the idea of families can be forever.

Before we were born to earth, we were spiritually borned and lived in the presence of our Heavenly Father.

"Before I formed thee in the belly I knew thee; and before thou camest forth out of the womb I sanctified thee, and I ordained thee a prophet unto the nations" (Jeremiah 1:5).

There we were taught, instructed, and given all things to help us in our journey here on the earth in order for us to return back to Him. Many have forgotten and gone a strayed because they don't remember the things that was taught and given to us in His presence.

The Lord when we left His presence, He wants to continue to communicate with us in order for Him to continue to help and guide us through our earthly journey and back to Him. We can continue communicate with Him through prayers, revelations, and personal revelations. The Lord has provided a plan for us to follow called *"The Plan of Salvation"* which can only be found in its fullness in the restored gospel of Jesus Christ here on the earth.

The Lord has already said, *"If any of you lack wisdom, let him ask of God, that giveth to all men liberally, and upbraideth not; and it shall be given him" (James 1:5).* He also said, *"Knock and it shall be open unto you, ask and it shall be given, seek and it shall be found" (Matthew 7:7).*

I invite everyone to give a try and prove it to yourself if these things are true. One thing that I can promise you that if you ask the Lord in prayer with the honest heart, the Lord will answer your prayer.

Hope and pray that this will give anyone a good start to ponder, study, learn and answer any questions that he has about the existence of God the Father and His only begotten Son Jesus Christ with the plan of salvation and the purpose of life and especially where we came from, why we're here and where we go after this life and how to **Live Learn Create and Relate** back to our Father in Heaven.

TESTIMONY

I testified that God our Heavenly Father lives. He loves us and He gave His only begotten Son to die for the sins of the world. The Atonement of Jesus Christ can save and return us to our Heavenly Father. Jesus is the Christ and the only way to Eternal Life. Jesus Christ is our Savior and Redeemer.

I testified Joseph Smith is a true prophet of God. He really saw God the Father and His Son Jesus Christ. I testified about that truth that they appeared to Joseph Smith in the sacred grove. I rated Joseph Smith the greatest prophet of all time save it to be Jesus Christ because He is the only begotten Son of God our Heavenly Father.

Joseph Smith is the Prophet of the restoration. All keys of the Priesthoods, Saving Ordinances, the Fullness of the Gospel of Jesus Christ and the Kingdom has been restored back on the earth through him. He has done so great even he seal his testimony with his blood just like our Savior Jesus Christ. He translated the Book of Mormon with the power of God. He organized the same Church Jesus Christ and His disciples organized in the ancients time back on earth which is the Kingdom of God on the earth also known The Church of Jesus Christ of Latter-day Saints.

I testified that if we ask it shall be given unto us, If we knock it shall be open unto us, If we seek we shall find it. I promised if we do these, God the Father will open up our understanding and our spiritual eyes will see the truth as He said. God never lie.

I pray that you and I may be bless that we may come to understand that when we were born we Lived, when we Lived we Learned, when we Learned we Created, when we Created we Related. Our purpose is to live happy and to learn as much as we can to return and live with God in Eternal Life.

In the sacred name of our Lord, Savior and Redeemer Jesus Christ Amen..

Printed in the United States
By Bookmasters